THE GOOD LIFE HANDBOOK

EPICTETUS' CLASSIC ENCHIRIDION

DR CHUCK CHAKRAPANI

THE STOIC GYM PUBLICATIONS
www.TheStoicGym.com

ABOUT THIS BOOK

This is a modern rendition of Epictetus' classic work, *The Handbook*, or *Enchiridion*. It answers the question, "How can we be good and live free and happy, no matter what's happening around us?" It is a concise summary of the teachings of Epictetus, as transcribed by his illustrious student, Flavius Arrian.

Epictetus, the great Stoic philosopher, was born around 55 CE in Hierapolis (present day Pamukkale, Turkey). Epictetus means 'slave' or 'acquired'. It is said that his parents sold him to Epaphroditos, a wealthy freedman and secretary to Nero. Eventually, Epictetus became a freedman himself and began to teach his philosophy.

This widely acclaimed modern rendition by Dr. Chuck Chakrapani brings ancient concepts to modern life.

www.TheStoicGym-com

Chuck Chakrapani/The Good Life Handbook - Gift edition
ISBN 978-0-920219-71-3

Contents

1 UNDERSTAND WHAT IS UNDER YOUR CONTROL 6

2 AVOID ONLY THINGS UNDER YOUR CONTROL 7

3 REMIND YOURSELF ABOUT THE NATURE OF THINGS 11

4 REMEMBER, THINGS CAN GO WRONG 11

5 IT IS YOUR JUDGMENTS THAT DISTURB YOU 12

6 YOU ARE NOT WHAT YOU OWN 13

7 ALWAYS BE PREPARED 15

8 WHAT WILL BE WILL BE 15

9 THE MIND IS NOT AFFECTED BY PROBLEMS 17

10 YOU HAVE THE RESOURCES TO COPE 17

11 YOU CAN'T LOSE WHAT YOU DON'T OWN 19

12 AVOID ANXIOUS THOUGHTS 19

13 IGNORE WHAT OTHERS THINK OF YOU 21

14 AVOID HAVING UNREALISTIC EXPECTATIONS 21

15 BE GENTLE IN YOUR DEALINGS 23

16 BE COMPASSIONATE 23

17 THINK OF YOURSELF AS AN ACTOR 25

18 EVERYTHING IS AUSPICIOUS 25

19 NO REASON TO ENVY OTHERS 27

20 DON'T REACT IMPULSIVELY 27

21 REMEMBER DEATH 29

22 BE PREPARED TO BE LAUGHED AT 29

23 DON'T SEEK OUTSIDE APPROVAL 31

24 DON'T COMPROMISE YOUR INTEGRITY 31

25 EVERYTHING HAS A PRICE 33

26 APPLY THE WISDOM TO YOURSELF 35

27 EVIL IS NOT INTENTIONAL 35

28 DON'T LET OTHERS CONTROL YOUR MIND 35

29 LOOK BEFORE YOU LEAP 37

30 KEEP YOUR SIDE OF THE RELATIONSHIPS.........39

31 PIETY IS NOT SEPARATE FROM SELF-INTEREST 41

32 YOU DON'T NEED TO KNOW THE FUTURE 43

33 BE TRUE TO YOURSELF 43

34 PAUSE AND CONSIDER THE CONSEQUENCES...................47

35 DON'T LET OTHERS STOP YOU 47

36 CONSIDER THE BIG PICTURE............................47

37 DON'T TRY TO DO THINGS BEYOND YOUR MEANS 49

38 CARE FOR YOUR MIND 49

39 UNDERSTAND YOUR NEEDS THE RIGHT WAY 49

40 CULTIVATE MODESTY AND SELF-RESPECT 49

41 ATTEND TO YOUR MIND.....................................51

42 TREAT YOUR CRITICS WITH COMPASSION 51

43 USE THE RIGHT HANDLE 53

44 YOU ARE NOT WHAT YOU HAVE.......................53

45 JUDGE THINGS PRECISELY 55

46 DON'T BRAG ABOUT YOUR PRINCIPLES 55

47 DON'T ADVERTISE YOUR SIMPLE LIFE 57

48 HELP AND HARM COME FROM YOU 57

49 YOUR ACTIONS ARE THE ONLY ONES YOU CAN BE...............58

50 STAND BY YOUR DECISION 59

51 DEMAND THE BEST OF YOURSELF NOW 61

52 EMPHASIZE ACTION OVER ARGUMENTS 63

53 REMEMBER THESE SENTIMENTS 65

THE STOIC GYM PUBLICATIONS 67

UNDERSTAND WHAT IS UNDER YOUR CONTROL AND WHAT IS NOT

1 UNDERSTAND WHAT IS UNDER YOUR CONTROL

Some things in life are under your control, and others are not.

What things are under your total control?

What you believe, what you desire or hate, and what you are attracted to or avoid. You have complete control over these, so they are free, not subject to restraint or hindrance. They concern you because they are under your control.

What things are not under your total control?

Your body, property, reputation, status, and the like. Because they are not under your total control they are weak, slavish, subject to restraint, and in the power of others. They do not concern you because they are outside your control.

If you think you can control things over which you have no control, then you will be hindered and disturbed. You will start complaining and become a fault-finding person. But if you deal with only those things under your control, no one can force you to do anything you don't want to do; no one can stop you. You will have no enemy and no harm will come to you.

If you want these substantial rewards in life you should be prepared to put in the effort. This means you may have to give up some things entirely and postpone others for now. If you attempt to get both what is under your control and what is not, you may end up getting neither. Therefore, you need to very clearly distinguish the two.

How do you tell the difference? Start by challenging everything that appears disagreeable. "You are only an appearance. Let me fully understand what you are." Then, using the distinction we talked about, examine it to see if it is under your total control. If it is not within your control, it is nothing to you; there's nothing to worry about.

AVOID ONLY THINGS UNDER YOUR CONTROL

2 AVOID ONLY THINGS UNDER YOUR CONTROL

We are ruled by our desires and aversions. When we desire something, we aim to get it. If we don't get what we desire, we feel disappointed.

When we are averse to something, we want to avoid it. If we end up getting what we don't want anyway, we feel unhappy.

If you desire and avoid only those things that are under your control, then you will not feel victimized by things you dislike. But if you resent unavoidable things like illness, misfortune, or death, that are not under your control, you are headed for disappointment.

Instead of showing dislike for what you cannot control, direct your dislike to things that are under your control but are contrary to your nature.

For now, suspend your desires. If you desire something outside your control you are bound to be disappointed. Even when we do control things, the outcome may not be what we desire.

Select carefully what you want to choose and what you want to refuse. Be disciplined and detached while making the choice.

REMIND YOURSELF OF THE NATURE OF THINGS

REMEMBER, THINGS CAN GO WRONG

3   REMIND YOURSELF ABOUT THE NATURE OF THINGS

When something is delightful or useful to you, remind yourself of its true nature. Start with small things. Suppose you like a ceramic cup you own. Tell yourself, "I love this ceramic cup." Then, if it breaks, you won't be disturbed because ceramic materials tend to break at some point.

Then try this with something that you consider a little more precious.

Eventually extend this understanding to everything. When you kiss your spouse or child, remind yourself that it is a mortal that you are kissing. Then you won't be too distraught should they be taken from you.

4   REMEMBER, THINGS CAN GO WRONG

Whenever you plan on doing something, mentally rehearse what can happen. If you are headed to a public swimming pool, remember people will splash, push, and yell. They may even steal your things. Or something else may happen to spoil your day. You will be at peace if you tell yourself, "Not only do I need a bath, but I also want to be calm and attuned to nature. Doing so would be impossible if I fell apart whenever something unexpected happened."

IT IS YOUR JUDGMENTS THAT DISTURB YOU

YOU'RE NOT WHAT YOU OWN

5   IT IS YOUR JUDGMENTS THAT DISTURB YOU

Events don't disturb people; the way they think about events does. Even death is not frightening by itself. But our view of death, that it is something we should be afraid of, frightens us.

So, when we are frustrated, angry or unhappy, let's hold ourselves responsible for these emotions because they are the result of our judgments. No one else is responsible for them.

When you blame others for your negative feelings, you are being ignorant. When you blame yourself for your negative feelings, you are making progress. You are being wise when you stop blaming yourself or others.

6   YOU ARE NOT WHAT YOU OWN

Don't be proud of the things you own. We could understand if your horse bragged about its beauty. But, don't you see that when you brag about your horse's beauty, you are taking credit for the horse's traits?

What quality belongs to you? The intelligent understanding of your first.

ALWAYS BE PREPARED

WHAT WILL BE WILL BE

7 ALWAYS BE PREPARED

When you are travelling by ship, you can go to the shore, enjoy the scenery, collect shells, or pick flowers. But when you are called back to the ship, you need to drop everything and hurry back, otherwise the ship may leave without you.

So it is with life. You have taken many responsibilities: your spouse, your children, and the like. But remember; you must be prepared to give up everything when called back.

8 WHAT WILL BE WILL BE

Don't wish for things to happen the way you would like them to. Rather, welcome whatever happens. This is the path to peace, freedom, and happiness.

THE MIND IS NOT AFFECTED BY PROBLEMS

YOU HAVE THE RESOURCES
TO COPE WITH EVERY CHALLENGE

9   THE MIND IS NOT AFFECTED BY PROBLEMS

Sickness is a problem for the body, not the mind, unless the mind decides that it is. Similarly, for lameness. It's the body's problem, not the mind's. If you practice attributing the correct source to problems you face, whatever happens, you will soon find that nothing that happens outside of you pertains to you.

10   YOU HAVE THE RESOURCES TO COPE WITH EVERY CHALLENGE

Remember that for every challenge you face, you have the resources within you to cope with that challenge. If you are inappropriately attracted to someone, you will find you have the resource of self-restraint. When you have pain, you have the resource of endurance. When you are insulted, you have the resource of patience. If you start thinking along these lines, soon you will find that you don't have a single challenge for which you don't have the resource to cope.

YOU CANNOT LOSE WHAT YOU DON'T OWN

AVOID ANXIOUS THOUGHTS

11 YOU CAN'T LOSE WHAT YOU DON'T OWN

You cannot really lose anything because you don't own anything in the first place. Not the stuff you have, nor your spouse, nor your property. They are given to you for temporary keep. So never say, "I have lost something." You just returned it. Your spouse died? (S)he was returned. You have lost your property? You returned it.

What if a thief stole your things? What does it matter to you who took what doesn't really belong to you? Think of all the things you have as things entrusted to you and you are free to enjoy them for a while. Think of it as a hotel stay. It is checkout time. Leave the hotel behind.

12 AVOID ANXIOUS THOUGHTS

If you want to make progress, stop feeling anxious about things. Don't think, "Unless I do such and such a thing, I might end up destitute." Or, "Unless I am strict with my subordinates, they will be undisciplined." Even if these things turn out to be true, it is better for you to be hungry than be anxious. It is better for your subordinates to be undisciplined than for you to be unhappy.

How do you train yourself not to be anxious? Start with small things. For example, you have spilled something on the carpet or something small is stolen from you. Say to yourself, "This is such a small price to pay for tranquility and peace of mind."

But remember, nothing is free. Things may not work out the way you want. When you choose not to be anxious, you do it in spite of your unfulfilled expectations. What you lose is what you pay for your peace of mind.

IGNORE WHAT OTHERS THIINK OF YOU

AVOID HAVING
UNREALISTIC EXPECTATIONS

13 IGNORE WHAT OTHERS THINK OF YOU

To make progress, you should be able to accept being seen as ignorant or naïve. Don't strive to be thought of as wise. Even if you succeed in impressing others as a wise person, don't believe it yourself.

You cannot be in agreement with nature and, at the same time, care about things outside your control. Caring about one thing comes at the expense of caring for the other.

14 AVOID HAVING UNREALISTIC EXPECTATIONS

You are being foolish if you expect your children, spouse, or friends to live forever. You don't have the power to make this happen.

It is equally naïve to expect everyone will be honest. It is not under your control, but in the control of others who may act honestly or dishonestly. Therefore, we are at the mercy of whomever has control over things we desire or detest.

You can, however, avoid disappointment and be free if you do not desire or avoid things that other people control.

BE GENTLE IN YOUR DEALINGS

BE COMPASSIONATE

15 BE GENTLE IN YOUR DEALINGS

Always conduct yourself as though you are at a formal dinner. If the dish has not reached you yet, don't be impatient. Wait your turn. When it comes around to you, reach out and take a modest amount. If it passes by you, don't try to pull it back.

If you act the same gentle and restrained way with your spouse, children, wealth, and status, you will be entitled to dine with the gods. If you go a step further and decline even what is given to you, you will not only be in the company of gods, but share their powers as well.

16 BE COMPASSIONATE

You may see people who are distraught and in tears because they had to part with their child or lost some material possession. Don't let the impression lead you to think that something bad happened to them. They are not upset by what happened to them but by their view of the situation.

However, be careful not to show disdain for their grief. Show them sympathy, use comforting words, and even share their misery outwardly. But make sure that you do not inwardly grieve with them.

THINK OF YOURSELF AS AN ACTOR

EVERYTHING IS AUSPICIOUS

17   THINK OF YOURSELF AS AN ACTOR

Consider yourself as an actor in a play. The nature of the play – whether short or long – is for the director to decide. The director will also decide whether your role is one of a poor person, a rich person, a cripple, a king, or a commoner. You as an actor do not decide these things.

Like an accomplished actor you need to perform the role assigned to you in life skillfully. The responsibility for deciding what role you play rests with someone else.

18   EVERYTHING IS AUSPICIOUS

If you come across anything you find to be an impediment to your progress – even if it be something you see as an inauspicious sign, something that will bring you bad luck, do not be upset by it. Examine the impression. It is of no significance to you. Nothing outside of you really pertains to you.

For you, every sign is auspicious, if you want it to be that way. Whatever happens, you can derive benefit from it.

NO REASON TO ENVY OTHERS

DON'T REACT IMPULSIVELY

19 NO REASON TO ENVY OTHERS

When you confine yourself to only those things that are under your control, you cannot be defeated.

Don't be fooled by outward appearances. People with more prestige, power, or some other distinction are not necessarily happier because of what they have.

There is no reason to be envious or jealous of anyone. If you lead a rational life, the good lies within you. Our concern should be our freedom, not titles and prestigious positions. The way to freedom is not to be too concerned about things we don't control.

20 DON'T REACT IMPULSIVELY

When someone provokes you, if you respond with anger or some other negative emotion, your mind is tricked into believing you are being harmed. So it is essential not to respond to impressions impulsively. Take some time before reacting. You will see you are in better control.

REMEMBER DEATH

BE PREPARED TO BE LAUGHED AT

21   REMEMBER DEATH

Whenever you face difficult situations in life, remember the prospect of death and other major tragedies that can and do happen to people. You will see that, compared to death, none of the things you face in life is important enough to worry about.

22   BE PREPARED TO BE LAUGHED AT

If you decide to live by lofty principles, be prepared to be laughed at by others. You may hear snide remarks: "Oh, here comes the philosopher!" or "Why are you so pretentious?"

Just ignore those comments. But make sure that you don't become pretentious. If you stick to your principles, people who make fun of you will eventually come around and may even admire you.

However, if you let others influence you to give up what you started, you will be ridiculed twice: firstly, for following these principles, and secondly, for giving them up.

DON'T SEEK OUTSIDE APPROVAL

DON'T COMPROMISE YOUR INTEGRITY

23 DON'T SEEK OUTSIDE APPROVAL

You compromise your integrity when you seek outside approval. Be satisfied that you live up to your rational principles. Be your own witness if you need one. You don't need any more witness than that.

24 DON'T COMPROMISE YOUR INTEGRITY

Don't let thoughts like, "People won't think well of me," or, "I will live in complete obscurity," bother you. Is living in obscurity bad? Do you decide how you will be recognized and whether you will get the job you deserve? Do you decide whether you will be invited to a party? No, you don't. How can what someone else chooses to do dishonor you?

You may say that unless you get a better job, you won't be able to help your friends. Whoever told you this is your responsibility? Who expects you to give others what you don't have?

If you can make money remaining honest, trustworthy, and dignified, by all means do it. But you don't have to make money if you have to compromise your integrity. A good friend would rather you didn't compromise your integrity than wish you gave him money.

You may then say that your community will be helpless unless you help. Your money can buy only material things for your community. So what? The community will benefit more by the presence of a lawful and loyal member than by material gifts. You cannot be much use to the community if you are shameless and corrupt.

EVERYTHING HAS A PRICE

25 EVERYTHING HAS A PRICE

Suppose someone else is preferred over you in public and their advice is sought in preference to yours, how should you respond? If he deserves it, you should be pleased for him. If he does not deserve it, don't get upset.

You cannot expect to get the same results he got unless you are prepared to do everything he was prepared to do. If you don't flatter, you will not have the advantages a flatterer will have. Those who are servile to their superiors will be rewarded differently from those who are not.

Everything has a price. For example, let's say that someone pays the retail price to get a head of lettuce. If you decide not to pay the price and go without the lettuce, you are not inferior to that person. He has the lettuce but you still have the money.

It's the same with social situations. If you are not invited to a party maybe it is because you didn't pay the price, such as flattering the host or doing things to be in her good books. So if you want to be invited, pay the bill and don't complain about the cost. But if you expect the benefits without paying the price you are not only greedy, you are being foolish.

What if you are not invited to the party? You did not do things you didn't want to do such as flattering the host. You have the advantage of not compromising your integrity.

APPLY THE WISDOM TO YOURSELF

EVIL IS NOT INTENTIONAL

DON'T LET OTHERS CONTROL YOUR MIND

26 APPLY THE WISDOM TO YOURSELF

When a friend breaks a cup, we are quick to say, "Oh, too bad. But these things happen." But when we break a cup we are easily upset. We need to accept what happens to us in the same spirit as we expect others to accept their lot.

We can apply this understanding to more serious things. When someone else's spouse or child dies, we commonly say, "Well, that's part of life." But when one of our own family members is involved we say, "Poor me. Why did this happen to me?"

Remember how wisely you understand when others face unfortunate situations. Apply the same wisdom when something unfortunate happens to you. Learn to accept whatever happens

27 EVIL IS NOT INTENTIONAL

No one sets up a target so others can miss it. Similarly, nature has not set up evil in this world so you can avoid it.

28 DON'T LET OTHERS CONTROL YOUR MIND

If your body was turned over to someone else, you would be ashamed and outraged. Should you not be equally ashamed when you turn over your mind to others so they can control it? Why do you let your mind be controlled by anyone who happens to criticize you? Why do you get confused and upset?

LOOK BEFORE YOU LEAP

29 LOOK BEFORE YOU LEAP

When you are about to undertake a project, consider not only what is involved now but what it would involve later. Otherwise you would plunge in enthusiastically at the beginning and end up quitting in disgrace when things get difficult later.

You would like to win at the Olympics? So would I. Who wouldn't? But consider what you need to do now and what you need to do later on before committing to it. You have to submit yourself to rigorous discipline, maintain a strict diet, avoid rich but tasty food, exercise long hours in inclement weather, refrain from drinking alcohol, and give up some of your social life. In short, you should hand yourself over to your trainer. It's not over yet. There will be times when you will dislocate your wrist, turn your ankle, and swallow sand. After all this, you may still end up losing. If, after considering all this, you still want to get involved, give it a go.

If you don't pause to consider what is involved, you will end up like a child: wrestler one minute, gladiator the next; actor one minute, musician the next. You will be like a monkey that imitates whatever comes its way, drawn by different things. You have not paid attention, and you have not thought things through. You are being casual and arbitrary.

Some people listen to a great philosopher and immediately want to be like him. Find out what you need to do to be a philosopher, just as you would find out what physical attributes you should have to become a pentathlete or a wrestler. Not everyone is cut out to do everything. If you become a philosopher you won't be able to drink and eat in the

same way you now do. You may have to stay up late, put up with pain, leave your family, be looked down upon by others, and suffer ridicule from strangers. Are you prepared to pay this price for serenity and freedom? If not, don't go near it. You can't be like a child playing different roles. You have to be one person and stick with the role you have chosen for —yourself.

KEEP YOUR SIDE OF THE RELATIONSHIPS

30 KEEP YOUR SIDE OF THE RELATIONSHIPS

Understand your connections to other people. In a relationship, it does not matter what the other person does. This man is your father. Your part of the relationship demands that you respect and support him and even tolerate his erratic behavior. He may be a bad father, but remember you are entitled only to a father, not to a good father.

Again, if you have a brother who is unfair, do not concern yourself with his behavior, but keep your behavior in tune with nature.

No one can hurt you unless you let them. You are hurt the moment you believe you are.

In all social dealings – as a father, mother, brother, friend, citizen, etc. – remember what your role is. It does not matter what the other person does.

PIETY IS NOT SEPARATE FROM SELF-INTEREST

31 PIETY IS NOT SEPARATE FROM SELF-INTEREST

If a divine order exists, as it does, we should hold correct beliefs about it. The order governs the world well and is just. We are here to be in tune with the natural order of things and welcome whatever happens as the product of the highest intelligence. This way you will neither blame the divine order nor think that it does not exist.

But first you should stop applying labels like "good" and "bad" to what is not under your control. The labels good and bad apply only to things under your control. If you consider anything beyond your control as good or bad, you will fail to get what you want and get what you don't want. You will blame the divine order and think of it as the cause of your troubles.

Everything in nature moves away from whatever is harmful and moves towards whatever is helpful. If you believe that someone has harmed you, you cannot love the offender or the offence. This is the reason why children who don't get what they want blame their parents, farmers curse the weather, and those who have lost their loved ones curse the gods.

Piety does not exist apart from self-interest. Therefore, when you practice using desire and aversion in the right way, you practice being pious.

Even so, it is never wrong to make sacrifice, offer drinks or other things to people, as long as it is done mindfully and not casually. Do not be miserly in your giving but be careful that you do not spend beyond your means either.

YOU DON'T NEED TO KNOW THE FUTURE

32 YOU DON'T NEED TO KNOW THE FUTURE

There is no need to consult astrologers to predict the future. We know that the events over which we have no control can be neither good nor bad. Since the future is not under our control it is nothing to us. Even if you believe in astrologers and consult them to predict the future, remember you are only learning about the future. Your problems can only be solved by reason.

No matter what the predictions for the future are, they do not override your obligations now to your friends, family, and country.

33 BE TRUE TO YOURSELF

Decide first what type of person you want to be and stick to it. Be the same person whether you are by yourself or with others. Here are some suggestions:

- Don't indulge in unnecessary chatter. Avoid gossiping about others. Speak with precision and speak about what really matters.
- If you want to influence your friends, do it by your example.
- Do not laugh too loud or too often.
- If possible, avoid taking oaths.
- Avoid fraternizing with people who don't share your values. Prolonged association with those with false ideas can only tarnish your thinking.
- Be moderate in meeting the needs of your body, be it food, drink, clothing, shelter, or household needs. Avoid ostentation and luxury.

BE TRUE TO YOURSELF

- Do not indulge in sexual impropriety. Don't be judgmental of those who do.

- Don't defend yourself if someone speaks ill of you.

- When you go to games, don't side with anyone except yourself. Wish for what happens to happen. Don't keep discussing the game long after it is over.

- When you go to listen to other people's lectures, remain attentive. Don't be disagreeable.

- When you go to meet someone, especially someone important, think of yourself as a dignified person and behave accordingly. You will get on with the other person, no matter what happens.

- When you seek to meet with people who are important, remember they may not be available; they may not want to see you or talk to you. If, considering all this, you still want to meet them, by all means go, if it is the right thing to do. But don't complain later that it was not worth it. To do so is the sign of an ordinary person at odds with life.

- In conversations, avoid talking at length about yourself. Just because you enjoy your exploits does not mean that others will. They will derive pleasure from hearing about them, not about you.

- Avoid trying to be funny.

- Avoid using profanities. If someone else uses profanities, and you are sure you are not out of line, you can point it out to the other person. Otherwise, it is enough to show your displeasure by being silent or looking uneasy.

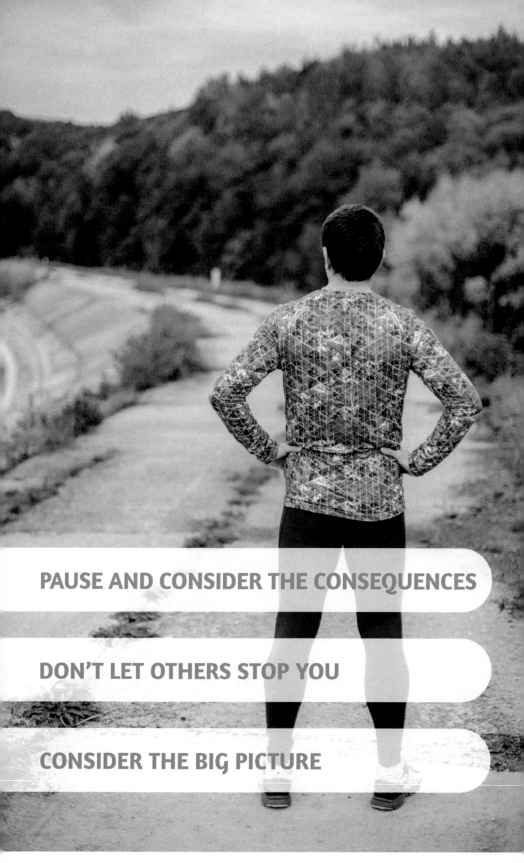

PAUSE AND CONSIDER THE CONSEQUENCES

DON'T LET OTHERS STOP YOU

CONSIDER THE BIG PICTURE

34 PAUSE AND CONSIDER THE CONSEQUENCES

When something looks pleasurable, don't get carried away by that impression. Take a minute and let it sink in. Then consider its effect at the time you experience pleasure and later. Will you still be happy or will you regret having indulged in something that's not good for you? Think about how good you would feel if you controlled yourself instead of being swayed by your first impression.

Take extra care to make sure you are not pushed around by the seductiveness of impressions. Think about how much better you will feel if you exercise self-control.

35 DON'T LET OTHERS STOP YOU

When you decide to do something you believe to be right, don't let others stop you, even if a majority of people disapprove of it. If it is a wrong thing to do, you should not do it in the first place. But if it is the right thing, then why care about what others think?

36 CONSIDER THE BIG PICTURE

Statements like, "It's day", and, "It's night", don't tell us what they mean if taken together. Similarly, serving yourself a large portion of healthy food may do good to your body, but would it help communal spirit if you did it at a dinner party? Be considerate of yourself, but also of others.

DON'T TRY TO DO THINGS BEYOND
YOUR MEANS

CARE FOR YOUR MIND AS MUCH AS
YOU DO YOUR BODY

UNDERSTAND YOUR NEEDS
THE RIGHT WAY

CULTIVATE MODESTY AND SELF-RESPECT

37 DON'T TRY TO DO THINGS BEYOND YOUR MEANS

Don't undertake to do things that are beyond your means. If you do, you will not only embarrass yourself but you will also miss an opportunity to do successful things that are within your means.

38 CARE FOR YOUR MIND AS MUCH AS YOU DO YOUR BODY

As you are careful not to step on a sharp object or sprain your ankle, so you should take care not to do any injury to your character. If you exercise caution when you act, you are less likely to damage your character.

39 UNDERSTAND YOUR NEEDS THE RIGHT WAY

Your shoe size is decided by the size of your feet. Use the same principle when dealing with other things, so you always understand what is right for your needs. Just as you would feel uncomfortable or even fall down when you use the wrong size shoes, so will you stumble if you exceed your limits in other things. Avoid excesses.

40 CULTIVATE MODESTY AND SELF-RESPECT

When girls come of age, they start receiving attention for their looks. As a result, they tend to become preoccupied with their appearances to the exclusion of other things. They should also concern themselves with cultivating modesty and self-respect.

ATTEND TO YOUR MIND

TREAT YOUR CRITICS WITH COMPASSION

41   ATTEND TO YOUR MIND

You should spend some time cultivating the body by eating, drinking, exercising, etc. However, spending too much time cultivating the body at the expense of cultivating the mind shows lack of refinement. While you should take care of your body, you should spend most of your time taking care of your mind.

42   TREAT YOUR CRITICS WITH COMPASSION

When someone criticizes you, they do so because they believe they are right. They can only go by their views, not yours. If their views are wrong, it is they who will suffer the consequences. Keeping this in mind, treat your critics with compassion. When you are tempted to get back at them, remind yourself, "They did what seemed to them to be the right thing to do."

EVERYTHING HAS TWO HANDLES

YOU ARE NOT WHAT YOU OWN

43   USE THE RIGHT HANDLE

Every situation in life comes with two handles: one by which you can carry it and the other by which you cannot. If your brother treats you poorly, the handle, "He harmed me", is the wrong handle to use. Instead, use the other handle, "He is my brother. We grew up together, even if what he does now may look hurtful." It is a better handle to carry the situation.

44   YOU ARE NOT WHAT YOU HAVE

Don't say, "I am richer, so I am better than you" or, "I am a more persuasive speaker, therefore I am better than you." If you are richer than me, you have more money than me; if you are a more persuasive speaker, you have better persuasive skills. But you are not your wealth, your diction, or any of the things you own.

JUDGE THINGS PRECISELY

DON'T BRAG ABOUT YOUR PRINCIPLES

45 JUDGE THINGS PRECISELY

If someone bathes quickly, don't say he doesn't bathe properly, say he bathes quickly. If someone drinks a lot, don't say he is a drunk, say he drinks a lot. Unless you know their reasons for their actions how can you be sure of your negative judgment of them? Not judging others too quickly will save you from misperceiving their actions.

46 DON'T BRAG ABOUT YOUR PRINCIPLES

Don't brag about the principles you follow in life. Don't even mention them to others. Instead, act according to those principles. In social situations, do not tell others how to behave.

If the conversation turns to philosophical principles, keep silent for the most part. Do not be in a hurry to show off what you think you know even before you have digested fully what you learned. If your silence is mistaken for ignorance and you are not upset by it, then it is a real sign of progress.

Sheep don't bring their owners grass to show how much they ate. Instead, they digest it and produce milk and wool. Similarly, don't make a show of principles you live by. Instead, live by them fully and show others by your actions how much you have learned and made it your own.

DON'T ADVERTISE YOUR SIMPLE LIFE

HELP AND HARM COME FROM YOU

47 DON'T ADVERTISE YOUR SIMPLE LIFE

If you have chosen a simple life, don't make a show of it. If you want to practice simplicity, do so quietly and for yourself, not for others.

48 HELP AND HARM COME FROM YOU

A wise person understands that help or harm come exclusively from herself. An ordinary person, on the other hand, looks for help or harm from others.

As you make progress, you will stop criticizing, blaming, or flattering others. You will not tell others how much you know or how important you are. If you are frustrated or disappointed, you will know you are responsible for it. If you are praised, you will be more amused than delighted. And you won't respond to criticisms. You will keep in mind you still have a long way to go.

Moreover, you will have no desires that are contrary to nature, and you will know you are in full control of your aversions. You do not care if others think you are naïve or stupid. Your only concern is to keep your focus on yourself, so you don't damage your progress.

YOUR ACTIONS ARE
THE ONLY ONES YOU
CAN BE PROUD OF

STAND BY YOUR DECISIONS

49 YOU ACTIONS ARE THE ONLY ONES YOU CAN BE PROUD OF

There is no point in being conceited about your ability to understand lofty philosophers. The only thing of importance is to follow the teachings so you can act according to nature. Only when you act according to nature, do you have something to be proud of.

50 STAND BY YOUR DECISION

Once you undertake to do something, stick with it and treat it as something that should be carried through. Don't pay attention to what people say. It should not influence you in any way.

DEMAND THE BEST OF YOURSELF NOW

51 DEMAND THE BEST OF YOURSELF NOW

How long will you put off demanding the best of yourself? When will you use reason to decide what is best? You now know the principles. You claim to understand them. Then why aren't you putting these principles into practice? What kind of teacher are you waiting for?

You are not a child anymore; you are fully grown. Don't be lazy and give excuse after excuse. If you continue to do this, your lack of progress may be hidden but, in the end, you will have lived a mediocre life.

Decide that you are an adult, and you are going to devote the rest of your life to making progress. Stick closely to what is best. If you are distracted by pleasure or pain, glory or disrepute, realize that the time is now. The game has started and waiting any further is not an option. Win or lose will be decided today. Use reason to meet every challenge.

EMPHASIZE ACTION OVER ARGUMENT

52 EMPHASIZE ACTION OVER ARGUMENTS

An argument has three parts. For example,

1. You should not lie;

2. Why you should not lie; and

3. Proof for the claim that you should not lie.

So, the third part is necessary for the second part which, in turn, is necessary for the first part. Of these three, the first part is the most important because it points to action. But we are often preoccupied with the third part and we continue to lie, and fail to act according to reason.

REMEMBER THESE SENTIMENTS

53   REMEMBER THESE SENTIMENTS

Have these sentiments handy in all circumstances.

Lead me, Zeus, lead me Destiny
To the goal I was long ago assigned
And I will follow without hesitation.
Even should I resist in a spirit of perversity,
I will have to follow nonetheless.

Whoever yields to necessity graciously,
We account wise in God's ways.

Dear Crito, if it pleases gods, so be it.

Anytus and Meletus can kill me, but they cannot harm me.

THE STOIC GYM PUBLICATIONS

FREE MAGAZINE
THE STOIC: THE JOURNAL OF THE STOIC GYM

THE STOIC is the official online magazine of The Stoic Gym. It is an applied magazine designed to bring high-quality articles on how to live a life of happiness, serenity, and freedom using Stoic principles. By subscribing, you can have the magazine delivered to your inbox, as soon as an issue is published. Subscribe. *It's FREE! https://www.thestoicgym.com/the-stoic-subscribe/*

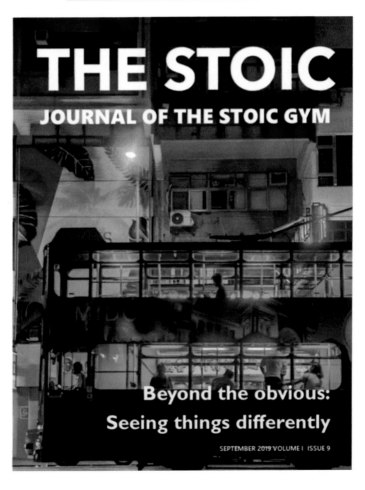

A 10-WEEK COURSE IN STOICISM

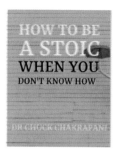

WITH 10 SPECIALLY CURATED EXERCISES, ONE FOR EACH WEEK

This unique 10-week training course is carefully designed to teach the essence of Stoicism. Each week's lesson starts with a big idea, followed by a discussion of how it works in practice, supported by a Stoic exercise to reinforce it, and a Stoic quote.

Each chapter contains two or three readings from ancient and modern Stoics and quotes for every day of the week.

The course covers:
- The foundational principles of Stoicism
- Four special skills we need to practice Stoicism
- Three disciplines we need to develop
- How to live a Stoic life
- How to enjoy the festival of life

The course includes 30 selected readings from the ancient and the modern Stoics and about 100 quotes from the ancient Stoics.

By the time you finish the course, you should have a solid understanding of the foundations of Stoicism.

Get your copy of the course today!

https://amzn.to/2PioGFc

YOUR GUIDE TO EVERYTHING STOIC

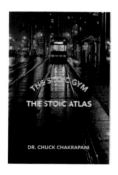

This short volume is an indispensable reference for modern Stoics. It covers the following topics:
- The Geography of Ancient Stoicism.
- The Geography of Modern Stoicism
- The Timeline of Ancient Stoicism
- The Timeline of Modern Stoicism
- Stoicism in Words, Pictures, and Numbers
- The History of Ancient Stoicism
- The History of Modern Stoicism
- An Outline of Ancient Stoicism
- An Outline of Modern Stoicism with pictures of Stoic sites (both ancient and modern) and photographs of the Modern Stoic movement

Both the online and the print editions are in full color, beautifully produced.

Get your copy now! https://amzn.to/2Wd8s1O

THE STOIC GUIDE TO A LIFE THAT FLOWS WELL

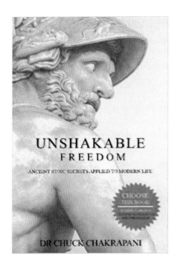

UNSHAKABLE FREEDOM How can we achieve total personal freedom when we have so many obligations and so many demands on our time? Is personal freedom even possible? Yes, said the Stoics, and gave us a blueprint for freedom. Dr. Chakrapani brings their teachings to the digital era.

WHAT READERS ARE SAYING

You'll "probably get through it in a few hours, enjoy the whole thing, and come away with an accurate and workable idea of Stoic philosophy. So please do just go and read it."

DONALD ROBERTSON, Book Reviews—Stoicism

"If you want to apply [the Stoic principles] right away, it is a wonderful book for that. This will help a lot of people. This is a gateway book."

Dr. GREGORY SADLER, Sadler's Honest Book Reviews.

Dr. Chakrapani has written a superbly helpful book."

BROGA, Amazon (UK)

The absolute best book by far ... is Unshakable Freedom by Chuck Chakrapani ... It explains Stoicism in an extremely accessible and easy to understand format. Highly rec-ommended. I've gifted it to quite a few people.

ILLEGALUTURN, reddit/r/stoicism

Available on all online bookstores eBook or paperback-
https://amzn.to/2O9jRNM

THE COMPLETE WORKS OF MARCUS AURELIUS IN TWO VOLUMES

This is the personal journal kept by the beloved Roman Emperor Marcus Aurelius. It was never meant for publication and yet, after his death, it has become probably the most widely read book on Stoic philosophy.

Meditations is a deeply moving personal journal which is uplifting and invigorating. https://amzn.to/2DqLLiT

While Meditations is one of the best-read Stoic books, not many of us know about Marcus' other writings: his personal letters and speeches. For the first time ever, Aurelius, the Unknown presents all his letters and speeches in a single volume. This book also includes a biographic sketch and several anecdotes from his life. A must-read for all fans of Marcus Aurelius. https://amzn.to/2DqLLiT

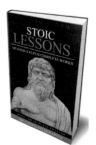

THE COMPLETE WORKS OF MUSONIUS RUFUS IN A SINGLE VOLUME

Musonius Rufus, the man who taught Epictetus, has something to say on everything. Far ahead of his time, he was a minimalist. vegetarian, proto-feminist, minimalist, and more.

https://amzn.to/2WbWwN1

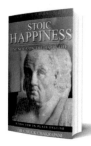

STOIC HAPPINESS

In this discourse, Seneca warns us that following the crowd is no way to be happy. He tells us that happiness is close at hand, by what means we can achieve it, and how to go about finding it. https://amzn.to/2I0mbVW

THE COMPLETE WORKS OF EPICTETUS
A set of five indispensable books

Stoic Foundations (Discourses Book 1) explains the basic tenets of Stoicism. If you are interested in Epictetus' teachings, this where you should start.

Stoic Choices is the plain English version of Discourses Book 2. It discusses what our choices are in life and how to make better choices.

Stoic Training is the third book of Discourses of Epictetus in plain English. Stoics did not only believe in theoretical knowledge but held it as critical that we practice what we learned.

Stoic Freedom (Discourses Book 4) focuses on freedom. Personal freedom is close to Epictetus' heart, and his rhetoric shines when he talks about it. But, what does a free person look like?

Stoic Inspirations includes a summary (or extracts) from the above four books by Arrian (Enchiridion) and The Golden Sayings of Epictetus. It also includes "fragments" (quotes) as well as a biography.

Available in print and digital editions from Amazon at https://amzn.to/2CGY3lk

Made in the USA
Las Vegas, NV
30 January 2022

42688839R00043